New Baby, New You

The Need to Know Guide to Postnatal Health and Happiness

How to Return to Exercise and Get Back in Shape After Giving Birth

DEBORAH BEARD

Discover more books and ebooks of interest to you and find out about the range of work we do at the forefront of health, fitness and wellbeing.

www.ymcaed.org.uk

Published by Central YMCA Trading Ltd (trading as YMCAed). Registered Company No. 3667206.

Central YMCA is the world's founding YMCA. Established in 1844 in Central London, it was the first YMCA to open its doors and, in so doing, launched a movement that has now grown to become the world's biggest youth organisation. Today, Central YMCA is the UK's leading health, fitness and wellbeing charity, committed to helping people from all walks of life – and particularly the young and those with a specific need – to live happier, healthier and more fulfilled lives.

Copyright © Central YMCA Trading Ltd 2013
All rights reserved.

ISBN: 1481912232
ISBN-13: 978-1481912235

All rights reserved. No part of this publication may be reproduced, stored in a retrieval system, or transmitted, in any form or by any means, without the prior permission of the publisher. This book is presented solely for educational and entertainment purposes. The author and publisher are not offering it as legal, medical, or other professional services advice. While best efforts have been used in preparing this book, the author and publisher make no representations or warranties of any kind and assume no liabilities of any kind with respect to the accuracy or completeness of the contents and specifically disclaim any implied warranties of merchantability or fitness of use for a particular purpose. Neither the publisher nor the individual author(s) shall be liable for any physical, psychological, emotional, financial, or commercial damages, including, but not limited to, special, incidental, consequential or other damages, resulting from the information or programs contained herein. Every person is different and the information, advice and programs contained herein may not be suitable for your situation. Exercise is not without its risks and, as such, we would strongly advise that you consult with your healthcare professional before beginning any programme of exercise, especially if you have, or suspect you may have, any injuries or illnesses, are currently pregnant or have recently given birth. The advice, information and guidance given in Central YMCA Guides is in no way intended as a substitute for medical consultation. As with any form of exercise, you should stop immediately if you feel faint, dizzy or have physical discomfort or pain or any other contra indication, and consult a physician.

CONTENTS

	About The Author	7
1	Now You're A Mum	9
2	Type of Labour	13
3	Before And After Your Six-Week Check	17
4	Finding The Right Exercise For You	21
5	Losing Your Baby Weight	35
6	Getting Out And About	37
7	Friends And Family	39
8	Sign Posting	41
9	Good Luck	43

ABOUT THE AUTHOR

Hi, I'm Deborah Beard and I'm a fitness instructor, tutor and assessor for YMCAfit – the UK's most established fitness training provider. I've worked in this incredible industry since 2003, teaching a range of courses aimed at fitness professionals. My speciality, however, is the fascinating topic of exercise and pregnancy.

I have also recently become a mum.

Indeed, as I write this book, my baby is 17 weeks old and so many of the feelings that you may be experiencing right now are still very fresh in my own mind too. I love exercise and, if you're anything like me, you're probably keen to get back in shape, while also still getting to grips with the day-to-day, and night-to-night, demands of life as a mum.

However, as I have taught over the years, this is a challenge that needs careful planning, it's one you can't rush into and one you need to approach in the right way. Hence the reason for this book. I want to make your return to fitness and to life as you, rather than as mum, a safe, enjoyable and achievable experience.

On YMCAfit's Exercise and Pregnancy course students learn about the physiological changes that take place and the effect that these will have on exercise, both during pregnancy and the postnatal period. It's a course that I love teaching and much of what we teach to physiotherapist and gym instructors will have huge relevance to mums, which is why I hope to relay much of it to you, in bite size chunks, over the coming pages.

This book will therefore explore the safest way for you to return to exercise after having your baby and help you to set realistic expectations for yourself. We will also look at how you can use your support network to become more active and we'll explore the benefits of getting out and about as much as possible with your new addition.

However, although I am a fitness professional, I am not a midwife or a doctor and although the exercise-related information you're about to read is based on real-life research, much of this book comes from my own personal opinion and experiences and should therefore not be used as a substitute for medical consultation. Indeed, my advice on this front is simple: consult your GP or other healthcare professional before commencing any programme of exercise, and stop immediately if you feel faint, dizzy or have any physical discomfort or pain. Other than that, have fun and go for it!

Enjoy the book.

Debs

1

NOW YOU'RE A MUM

WHAT HAS HAPPENED TO YOUR BODY AND WHAT WILL HAPPEN NOW?

As you are all too aware, your body went through some incredible changes during your pregnancy, many of which will now need to be considered as you recover from giving birth.

Of course in the early days you'll feel like you have been in a boxing ring. Indeed, even if you had a straightforward, natural labour, you will have put in a massive physical and emotional effort to bring your baby into the world. I remember finding it very difficult just to get from my hospital bed to the shower for the first time and to move from one room to another once I returned home.

The type of delivery you had will have a huge bearing on how soon you can return to exercise and there will be more on this in a later chapter, but whether Caesarean or vaginal, be prepared for the physical restrictions to last for a while and accept that even walking a short distance will feel like a marathon.

Regardless of this, the one form of exercise you can and should do with immediate effect are your pelvic floor contractions. I will refer to this again and again over the coming pages because exercising this muscle group really is vital for a good recovery and for prevention of continence issues later in life.

During your pregnancy, your body has been doing a wonderful thing. During your labour, your body has done yet another wonderful thing so be patient and kind to it during your postnatal period. Don't attempt to replicate those celebrities you'll inevitably see in the media who seemingly spring back into shape immediately. It is completely normal for you to still look pregnant for some time after birth.

For starters, it takes 10 to 12 days just for your uterus to shrink back to its original size. Add to that the fact that your body will have been storing fat reserves in preparation for breastfeeding and it's fair to say that you will be carrying normal, natural and expected extra weight for a little while yet.

Many women like to weigh themselves on the day of the birth, both before and after, as it's the most dramatic weight loss you will ever experience. However, once your milk comes in around days four to six, you can expect those scales to start creeping back up. Bearing all this in mind, I'd say that you're best off staying away from the scales altogether!

As well as all the physical changes, there will be emotional changes to consider too. You may have heard of the baby blues, which is a feeling of low mood, tearfulness and exhaustion. In most women, this usually happens around days four to six, which coincides with your milk supply coming in. These feelings are generally linked to a crash in the pregnancy hormones and a surge of the breastfeeding ones in their place, so it's quite understandable that your poor body and mind are all over the place at this life-changing time.

The baby blues can usually last a few days, but if your symptoms last for longer or if you feel that things are becoming unbearably desperate, then it may be the sign of postnatal depression and I would advise that you talk openly to your partner, midwife, health visitor or GP about it. They can point you towards appropriate help or support.

Of course, this is a truly magical time and you will undoubtedly find yourself staring at your baby for hours and marvelling at the miracle of human life. My husband and I still regularly look at our daughter in awe and wonder how on earth we created such a perfect little human. Enjoy these times and be proud of what you have achieved.

You may well find that exercise is the last thing on your mind, even if you were a gym addict before you had your baby. However, you are probably reading this book because you want to get back to exercise and over the coming pages we'll look at the best way do this, with one key thing in mind: a *gradual* approach is the best way forward. Remember, it took nine months for your body to change, so expect it to take nine months to get back to how it was.

Central YMCA Mums' Health Guides

2

TYPE OF LABOUR

VAGINAL DELIVERY

The most common and medically preferred option for bringing a new human being into this world is via a natural, vaginal birth. As women, we are biologically designed to give birth in this way and clearly we have been doing so for thousands of years. However, complications can occur and thankfully when they do we now have highly skilled medics on hand to give us the treatment and intervention we, and our babies, need.

Common interventions in childbirth include the use of forceps, curved, tong-like instruments that allow the doctor or midwife to make contact with the baby inside and assist him or her out. Another common intervention is the ventouse, an odd looking piece of equipment that is attached to the baby's head via a suction cup, essentially acting as a vacuum and allowing him or her to be pulled into the world. An episiotomy, meanwhile, is when the medical professional makes a surgical cut to the vagina to create enough room for the baby to come out. As you can imagine, or remember, there will be a great deal of soreness associated with an episiotomy cut and you will have a painful perineum (the muscle between the vagina and the anus) for quite some time after labour. The cut will need to be stitched and healing can take a while. Similarly, women sometimes tear their perineum naturally during childbirth which can also require stitches. Importantly, in these circumstances you will need to wait until you are feeling less tender in the vaginal area before you start any exercise programme. Some women, however, will not experience much pain at all in this area after giving birth, but it is still advisable to take your time before becoming too active.

As I mentioned earlier, just walking from one room to another can prove quite challenging for a lot of mums after giving birth. I remember overdoing the walking in the first week and my pelvic floor muscles didn't like it at all! You will of course also be bleeding quite heavily at this time. This blood and discharge loss is called lochia, it can last anywhere between two to six weeks and usually starts off heavy and then becomes gradually lighter over the days and weeks that follow. It's very important that you use pads rather than tampons during this time to reduce the risk of infection.

It is not advisable to undertake any vigorous activity during this time as you are still at risk of haemorrhaging during these early days. By doing pelvic floor exercises, not only will you be working on strengthening the muscles, but you will also be encouraging blood flow to the area which will in turn promote healing. To learn how to carry out pelvic floor exercises, skip ahead to the Types of Exercise chapter where you will find a clear explanation of how to do them.

CAESAREAN SECTION

During this type of labour, a cut into the abdominal area is made and the abdominal muscles are separated, not cut as is often incorrectly assumed.

However, even though these muscles are not cut, there are many other layers of tissue that are, so this clearly makes for a major and involved operation. Some people see this as the easy option and you will often hear the phrase 'too posh to push', but this procedure, and recovery from it, is by no means a breeze. Indeed, the recovery from a C-section is generally much longer than that of a vaginal delivery. As for exercise, it is advised that you do not drive for at least six weeks after a caesarean, so returning to an exercise regimen is obviously out of the question.

However, as with a vaginal delivery, it's never too early to start those pelvic floor squeezes. It's also good to carry out some static abdominal contractions, which will work your deep, stabilising core muscles. After a C-section, it's normal to feel numb for quite a while so you may not be able to feel yourself working your abdominal muscles and pelvic floor, but if you are confident you knew how to contract them before then continue with it even if you can't feel much. I remember feeling so disappointed in the early days after birth as I really couldn't tell if I was engaging my pelvic floor or not!

As a general rule of thumb, regardless of the type of delivery, it is advisable to wait until you have had your six-week check with your GP before embarking on a specific exercise programme. A C-section delivery requires a longer recovery period, usually about 10 to 12 weeks, but your GP will discuss this with you.

In the next chapter, we will look at what activities are safe to carry out before your six-week check and how to progress gradually thereafter.

Central YMCA Mums' Health Guides

3

BEFORE AND AFTER YOUR SIX-WEEK CHECK

There are two key postnatal periods with which you need to be familiar: the immediate postnatal period – the first six weeks after birth – and the extended postnatal period – six weeks post-birth and onwards. Put simply, you should not start a vigorous exercise programme in the immediate postnatal period. However, there are a few activities that you could carry out at this time and we will come on to these shortly.

After you have had your baby you will see a midwife and a health visitor in the first few weeks and then you and your baby will have a scheduled check-up with your GP at around six weeks. During this visit, your baby will be examined and your GP will ask you a variety of questions about how you have been recovering. As we've already stated, your body will have gone through an awful lot over the nine months of your pregnancy, and we won't go in to too much detail here, but one affected area that we do need to concern ourselves with are the changes in your abdominal muscles.

During pregnancy the rectus abdominis (your six-pack) muscles lengthen and separate in order to accommodate your growing foetus. It takes time for these muscles to return to normal after birth and it's important that you do not do any abdominal curls or sit-ups whilst they are still separated because you will strengthen them in their lengthened position, and hinder their recovery. Before you start doing any sit-ups or abdominal curls, you will need to ask your doctor to do a 'rec check', whereby they feel your abdominal muscles whilst you are lying on your back. By doing this, they will be able to tell you if your abdominal muscles have returned to their pre-pregnancy state. An exercise and pregnancy instructor should also be able to carry out this check for you. It's not standard for GPs to do this at the six-week check, so make sure you ask them to do it for you. Once the doctor has confirmed that your rectus abdominis has returned appropriately, then you can start a gradual, progressive abdominal programme, which will be covered in a little more detail shortly. However, even if your muscles haven't returned to their normal position, you can still perform static contractions for the abdominals, which may even help this area of the body go back to normal sooner. A description of how to do these contractions can be found in the Types of Exercise section.

As discussed earlier, if you have had a C-section, you will have to wait a while longer before you can return to exercise. It's usually around 10 to 12 weeks so speak to your doctor about your individual situation and follow his or her advice.

HIGH IMPACT EXERCISE

There is no doubt that your pelvic floor will have been a topic of conversation during your pregnancy and this will continue to be the case for a while yet. This is another change in the body that you will need to be aware of if you are keen to return to exercise. Your pelvic floor muscles are structured like a hammock that runs from your pubic bone at the front of your body to your coccyx (tailbone) at the bottom of your spine. These muscles literally are the floor of your pelvis and they have an important job to perform by keeping you continent. Because of where these muscles are positioned, they constantly have gravity working against them when you are in a standing position. During pregnancy, a rapidly growing foetus is adding more pressure and the hormones are working to make this area of your body more elastic in preparation for childbirth. Quite understandably, it is not a good idea to carry out high impact exercise whilst you are pregnant as this will apply even more pressure to the area. If you have had a vaginal delivery, the baby has to pass through these muscles on his journey into the world. So, all this considered, your pelvic floor muscles will have had quite a workout and you'll need to take good care of them.

Limiting high impact exercise in the first three months after labour is also advisable to allow the pelvic floor time to recover appropriately. Even if you had a C-section it's important to remember that the weight of your growing baby has been pressing down on your pelvic floor for nine months and the muscle group will be weakened, especially if you have had a baby before.

Startlingly, statistics show that 33% of mums still suffer from stress incontinence (leaking of urine) some nine months after birth [Incontinence survey on 1423 women aged 16-54. Gallup poll 1994]. Worryingly many of these mums just continue to suffer in silence as they think that it is the norm after having a baby.

The good news is that, with work, the pelvic floor can return to its previous strength and function. As I mentioned earlier, my baby is four months old and in the first week after her birth, I couldn't believe how weak my pelvic floor felt. I was convinced that it would never go back to normal despite my knowledge of the subject. I had spent nine months of pregnancy avidly working on my pelvic floor, but I had a particularly forceful labour and I also had an episiotomy. This meant that the muscle group had quite a bit of recovering to do so I had to be very patient and disciplined with my exercises.

BREASTFEEDING AND INTENSITY LEVELS

If you are breastfeeding your baby, you need to consider the intensity levels when exercising. During pregnancy, a hormone called relaxin is released and its job is to increase elasticity in the ligaments around the pelvis to allow it to widen for childbirth. However, the body isn't quite clever enough to restrict this hormone to the pelvic area, so instead it affects all joints. This can lead to injury if you over-do it because joints move more than they are naturally designed to do.

Although this is primarily a pregnancy hormone, it is still present whilst breastfeeding and therefore it's important that you limit high impact exercise and advanced stretching to avoid irreparable damage to the joints and ligaments. It is also thought that exercising at a very high intensity can affect the taste of breast milk, making it bitter. However, there isn't any conclusive evidence to prove this and the intensity would have to be extreme for this even to be a factor to consider. If this is a concern for you, then ensure that you breastfeed your baby before a training session. Having empty breasts will also make you feel more comfortable when exercising. It is also very important for you to remain well hydrated whilst breastfeeding as dehydration can affect your milk production. If you are exercising, you will need extra fluids to ensure your milk is not compromised.

EXERCISES YOU CAN DO IN THE IMMEDIATE POSTNATAL PERIOD (BEFORE YOUR SIX-WEEK CHECK)

DO

- Pelvic floor contractions (fast and slow)
- Static abdominal contractions
- Walk

DON'T

- Run or do any other high impact exercise such as jumping or bouncing
- Swim (unless your bleeding has stopped, due to the risk of infection)
- Do any advanced stretching (because of the relaxin)

EXERCISES FOR THE EXTENDED POSTNATAL PERIOD (AFTER YOUR SIX-WEEK CHECK)

There isn't a specific list of exercises that you should start doing once you are back in action as it very much depends on your exercise history and, most importantly, what you enjoy. If you enjoy a particular type of exercise or sport then you are far more likely to adhere to it. However, consider what we have discussed already when making your exercise choices: it's important to adopt a gradual approach. In the next chapter, we will look at the different types of exercise you could include, with a few examples of each.

4

FINDING THE RIGHT EXERCISE FOR YOU

Different people have different motivations for exercise. Some people do it because they love the feeling that they get after their session, others may do it for weight loss, gain or maintenance and some may do it for the feeling of escapism that they get, or even for social reasons. It may therefore be wise for you to analyse your own motivations for exercise and then you can remind yourself of this when necessary.

I once read in a running magazine that when you are trying to make excuses for not training, consider the fact that you never regret going for a run, but you will regret not going. I often remind myself of this if I am trying to talk myself out of an exercise session.

I am a fitness instructor so if I didn't practise what I preach then I would be a hypocrite, but I genuinely do feel that exercise makes a huge difference to my wellbeing. If I don't exercise for a few days, I start to feel quite cranky and lethargic, but once I have blown the cobwebs away by going for a walk or a run then I feel immeasurably better. Clearly, with a newborn baby, you have to want to exercise otherwise it may be difficult to make it a priority. One of your top priorities may be getting some sleep, but you'll be surprised how much a stroll around the block can make you feel better.

With a new baby, you are exercising in the non-traditional sense as you are regularly carrying them around. As they get bigger, you are working harder.

I am not suggesting that you use your baby as a dumbbell, but just through looking after them day-to-day you will inevitably do a fair amount of lifting and carrying. It is not unusual to find yourself getting a bit out of breath when you are playing with your baby, or when using a baby carrier. Indeed, you might feel like you are pregnant again as the sensation of carrying around all that extra weight comes back to you. These bonus activity sessions will do you no harm at all, but you will need to think about your posture.

One of the classes that I teach is Pilates which requires a strong awareness of posture. Before I had a baby, I used to look at the way friends and family tended to their children and criticise their posture, but now I am one of them. When you are changing a nappy, you are often kneeling on the floor with your shoulders hunched over. When you are carrying your baby around the house and trying to put things away in the cupboard at the same time, your spine isn't usually in the optimum position and even when you are pushing the pram outside, you may find yourself hunched over the handle bars. If you can get to a Pilates or yoga class, or any class that focuses on posture and core control, it may help you to become more aware of how you could correct the poor positions that you are getting yourself into on a daily basis.

Generally speaking, during pregnancy the muscles of the upper back become lengthened and weak and the muscles of the chest become short and tight. This is due to the weight of your growing breasts pulling you forward. In order to counteract this, it's important to perform back strengthening exercises during and after pregnancy and we will look at some specific exercises shortly.

There are four core components of fitness that should be included in any exercise regimen in order to create a balanced approach:

- Cardiovascular
- Muscular strength and muscular endurance
- Flexibility
- Motor skills

Cardiovascular

This type of activity will get your heart rate up and make you feel out of breath. The scientific definition is the ability to take in, transport and utilise oxygen. Cardiovascular, or CV, exercise encompasses anything that uses the large muscle groups, such as those found in your legs and bottom. Some examples of cardiovascular exercise include:

- Walking/jogging/running
- Cycling
- Aerobics
- Swimming

BENEFITS

By performing 30 minutes of CV activity five to seven days a week at a moderate intensity you will reduce your risk of cardiovascular disease, some cancers and type 2 diabetes. The 30 minutes can be accumulated throughout the day and can be broken down into three 10-minute bouts of activity, making it more achievable. However, to prevent obesity, 45 to 60 minutes of physical activity a day may be required. As a new mum, it is not advisable to jump straight to a 60 minute CV session as soon as you have had your six-week check. The goal at this stage should be to do a little bit of activity each day to a comfortable level. When choosing your exercise, bear in mind the physiological changes that we talked about in the previous chapter.

Having a good level of CV fitness will enable you to keep up with your fast approaching toddler, so make this type of exercise a stepping stone to your long-term goal! More information on the importance of physical activity can be found on the Department of Health Website (www.dh.gov.uk).

MUSCULAR STRENGTH AND MUSCULAR ENDURANCE

This type of exercise improves the capability of individual muscle groups by improving their strength (the ability to control heavy loads for short periods of time) or their endurance (to control moderate loads over an extended period of time). The following are a few examples of muscular strength and endurance exercises:

- Resistance machines in the gym
- Free weights (barbells and dumbbells)
- Yoga
- Body conditioning/body sculpt classes

By carrying out these types of exercises two to three times a week, you will reduce your risk of osteoporosis, increase your resting metabolic rate (this means you will burn more calories when you are not exercising), your shape and posture will improve, the strength and endurance of specific muscles will increase, and you will have an improved ability to carry out everyday tasks, such as pushing the pram and picking up your baby.

As delightful as these benefits are, lifting heavy loads with a weak pelvic floor is not a good idea, so it is best to wait until you are recovered before embarking on a heavy resistance training programme.

FLEXIBILITY

This is the amount of movement available around a joint. It's the ability of a muscle to lengthen to the level that it is designed to. You will likely have seen some people who can't touch their toes or reach around their back to fasten their bra strap. This is an example of poor flexibility. Flexibility is challenged in yoga and Pilates classes and there should be a flexibility section included in the cool down of any class or gym programme. To gain the following benefits, stretching should take place five to seven days a week. Some of the benefits of keeping flexible are improved posture, increased range of movement, maintenance or development of muscle length, and relaxation.

As we mentioned earlier, relaxin will still be floating around your system after you have given birth, and it will be present even longer if you are breastfeeding, so it's important that you only carry out stretches that last for a short while (10-15 seconds). Some of the stretches that take place in a yoga class, for example, can be lovely but quite intense and although you may be pleasantly surprised that you seem more flexible than you used to be, over-stretching will not be good for the long-term health of your joints.

MOTOR SKILLS

Motor skills is the collective term given to balance, agility, coordination, power, reaction time and speed. This component of fitness is highly important for skill-related sports such as football, rugby, boxing and dancing. However, it's important for us all to work on our motor skills. You will be challenging them by taking part in team sports, joining an aerobics class or a dynamic yoga session. Some of the benefits include improved coordination (a necessary skill with a newborn), improved proprioception (an example of this is climbing stairs and being spatially aware), faster reaction times and improved balance (thus decreasing the risk of falls).

The good news is that your motor skills are challenged automatically by taking part in most exercise so you shouldn't need to make a specific effort to incorporate this into your exercise plan. Consider that during pregnancy, your centre of gravity and balance will have changed dramatically. You will probably remember bumping into things and getting stuck in small spaces in the later stages of pregnancy. Although your bump will no longer be there, your balance may still be affected, so bear this in mind before joining an advanced choreography dance class!

Although it is important to aim to work on each of these components of fitness, the best advice I can give is to take up an exercise that you enjoy. So many people join a gym each year, pay a monthly membership and never go because they don't like it. Realistically, exercising with a new baby will be a bit of a juggling act that will require precious time and effort, but the physical and emotional rewards will be worth it.

Let's now have a look at the different ways you can incorporate some exercise into your new life.

EXERCISING AT HOME

You will be surprised how much you can do at home, even if you only have a small space. You could, for instance, create your own stepper machine by repeatedly climbing your stairs, giving you a great cardiovascular workout. You can also do squats and lunges anywhere in the house, not to mention press-ups, challenging your muscular strength and endurance. An additional benefit is that you can do these exercises whilst your baby is near you, or when they are asleep. Read on to discover a few workout ideas that are great to carry out in the comfort of your own home.

EXERCISING OUTSIDE

If you are short on babysitters, you will need to take your baby out with you. Walking outside with the pram is great exercise for you and research shows that fresh air helps a baby to sleep better. You will be amazed at how much a stroll around the block will clear your sleep-deprived head, making you feel much better. Realistically, it is not safe for you to use the pram as an exercise tool, but the sheer effort of pushing your baby up a hill whilst walking at speed will challenge even the fittest of people. If this is your second child, a double buggy is double the workout!

EXERCISING ALONE OR IN A GROUP

If you exercised before your pregnancy, you may have preferred group exercise over exercising alone, or vice versa. There should be a range of specific postnatal classes in your local area that you can join. This is a great way of meeting other new mums and more often than not these groups involve activity with the pushchair, so there will be no babysitters required.

However, providing you have had your six-week check and have been signed off by the doctor, you can take part in your usual exercise classes. Doing this can make you feel like your old self again and it's a great way to switch off and have some time for yourself. You will need to ensure that you listen to the easier alternatives that the class instructor offers, particularly if you are only just outside of your immediate postnatal period. If the instructor isn't offering you alternatives, don't be afraid to ask as it's their job to ensure that all members of their class are catered for. However, not all instructors are exercise and pregnancy trained so you may need to do your research before assuming that your usual instructor will know how to accommodate you.

If you prefer to exercise alone, and you have had your six-week check you can do any exercise that you feel comfortable with as long as you use caution with impact in the first three months. Some people love the idea of being led by an instructor as they need the motivation, whereas others prefer solitary training so that they can get lost in their own thoughts, or switch off. Throughout life, you may find that your preferences change. Any activity that you take part in is better than doing nothing at all.

People often assume that to get fit and gain the health benefits of exercise, there has to be blood, sweat and tears involved. This is simply not true and, in fact, research has shown that you reap far more health benefits by being generally more active each day rather than going to the gym three times a week, but being sedentary for the rest of the time. So if you don't feel ready for structured exercise just yet, don't worry, just use the stairs instead of the lift, walk instead of drive, do your pelvic floor contractions instead of just standing in a queue and go to the supermarket rather than doing your shopping online.

Remember, the recommended amount of daily activity can be accumulated in three 10-minute chunks if necessary, so every little helps. Below are some exercise examples to get you moving. You can also find more information on these exercises, together with some short videos at our YMCA Mums' Health magazine:

http://www.pocketmags.com/viewmagazine.aspx?titleid=1270&title=YMCA+Mums'+Health

CV EXERCISE

As discussed, CV exercise is anything that gets you out of breath.

You can always find an excuse to get out and about with the pram rather than taking the car. In order to add an extra challenge to that stroll, why not try walking intervals.

WALKING INTERVALS

- Walk for five minutes at a moderate pace until you feel warmed up
- Walk as fast as you can for two minutes
- Walk at moderate pace for one minute to recover
- Repeat these intervals five to eight times so that you have been working out for about 20 to 30 minutes in total

Depending on your fitness level and how far postnatal you are, you could always change the walking intervals to running intervals instead. However, you will need to consider the temperature outside as running towards the wind with an outward facing pram may cause too much of a chill for your baby who will not be able to regulate his or her body temperature as well as you can. Also, please consider the safety of running with a pram or a buggy; specific buggies are available for activity and all of them include some form of strap to attach you to your buggy. You can't be too careful, so don't take any risks.

USE THE STAIRS

When you are out with the pram, it's not practical for you to use the stairs in shopping centres or at stations. However, if you have your baby in a sling/baby carrier then there is no reason not to take the stairs. With the added weight attached to you, it'll be like walking stairs with dumbbells. If you have stairs at home, you can use them as a good CV workout without the need to leave the house. Walk up and down the stairs as many times as you can. You can make this harder by climbing two stairs at a time. Once again though, don't push yourself too hard or take any risks if you are carrying your baby.

If you belong to a gym, there will be a range of CV equipment for you to use such as treadmills, cross-trainers, bikes and rowers. There may also be classes for you to attend that will challenge your CV fitness.

MUSCULAR STRENGTH AND MUSCULAR ENDURANCE EXERCISES

These types of exercise are often referred to as toning or conditioning. If you are pushed for time, it's a good idea to work the largest muscle groups of the body such as the chest, legs, bottom and back. This is because larger muscle groups will burn more calories and the majority of the time you will also be working some of the smaller muscles inadvertently. Classes such as sculpt, 'legs, bums and tums' or body conditioning will challenge your muscular strength and endurance.

SQUATS – 2 SETS OF 25

This exercise works your thighs and bottom.

1. Stand with your feet hip width apart or slightly wider with the feet facing forwards or slightly outwards
2. Your heels should remain down throughout the exercise
3. Bend the knees and the hips, lowering until the knees are at 90 degrees
4. Maintain a neutral position throughout the movement
5. Keep the head up and the eyes facing forward
6. Ensure that the knees travel in line with the feet and stay behind the toes
7. Push strongly with the legs to regain an upright position but without locking your knees

LUNGES – 2 SETS OF 25

This exercise works your thighs and bottom.

1. Position your feet hip width apart with the toes facing forwards
2. Step directly forward with one leg and then lower towards the floor
3. The step should be a sufficient distance to enable both knees to bend at a right angle without the trailing knee contacting the floor
4. Keep the body upright and the toes pointing forwards
5. Drive back with the leg to the starting position, then repeat alternating the leading leg
6. Maintain the feet at hip width apart whilst alternating the stepping action. This helps to maintain a stable base
7. Relax the shoulders and arms

Press-ups – 2 sets of 12

This exercise works your chest muscles and the back of your arms.

1. Come down to the floor so that your hands and the bottom of your thighs are in contact with the floor (be careful not to put pressure on your knee cap)
2. Position the hands shoulder width and a half apart
3. Bend the elbows to lower the body towards the floor
4. Straighten elbows without locking out the joint, to lift the body up
5. Keep the spine as neutral as possible and the shoulders away from the ears

You can make this exercise easier by bending your knees more so that you are in a box position, or harder by lifting your knees from the floor and resting on your toes

Back Extension – 2 sets of 12

This exercise works the muscles in your back.

1. Lie on your tummy
2. Place the hands either at the side of the thighs or at the side of the head. The position of the hands will change the intensity
3. Raise the head and shoulders up
4. Keep looking forwards and slightly down as if you are looking into a pool of water
5. Gently lower back down to the floor
6. Avoid lifting too high. Just a few inches off the floor is enough of a challenge
7. Keep your feet in contact with the floor

Pelvic floor

I have already explained the importance of the pelvic floor muscles and their role in pregnancy and childbirth and here is just a little more detail about how they are structured and most importantly, how to carry out the exercises that strengthen them.

Two layers make up the pelvic floor, one superficial and one deep. Each layer is made up of two particular types of muscle fibre:

Slow twitch – These fibres are slow to fatigue. They have the ability to produce a comparatively long contraction, though not a very strong one.

Fast twitch – These fibres have the ability to produce immediate, strong contractions.

The combination of these two types of muscle fibre in the pelvic floor enable it to maintain tone and endurance and also to respond to sudden rises in abdominal pressure such as coughing, sneezing, laughing and exercising.

HOW TO CARRY OUT PELVIC FLOOR CONTRACTIONS

1. In any position, sitting, standing or lying, have the legs slightly apart
2. Draw up and close the back passage/anus as if to stop yourself passing wind
3. Draw up and close the front passage as if to stop the flow of urine
4. Squeeze and lift up inside the vagina
5. Keep breathing naturally
6. Hold for a few seconds and then let go slowly
7. Try to increase the length of hold for 10 seconds
8. Repeat up to 10 times an hour

Once the technique of the pelvic floor exercises becomes familiar, quick one-second contractions can be practised in addition to the slow, held ones.

One test that indicates whether your pelvic floor strength is adequate is to try and stop the flow of urine mid-stream. However, this test should only be carried out occasionally due to the risk of retaining stale urine which could cause infections. A more fun test is to carry out a star jump on a trampoline at the same time as coughing, and seeing if you remain completely dry!

The slow and fast pelvic floor contractions outlined here target both the deep and superficial muscles and they should be practised regularly – approximately 100 times a day. Aim to set yourself reminders by associating pelvic floor contractions with everyday activities such as breastfeeding your baby, making up their bottle or flushing after you have been to the loo. Another good tip is to put little red reminder stickers in places that you regularly visit, such as the fridge, the bathroom or even the car.

STATIC ABDOMINAL CONTRACTIONS

If you have some experience of exercise, you may be familiar with core stability exercises, which work your transverse abdominis together with other muscles of the trunk. Basically speaking, this is your deepest abdominal muscle, positioned closest to the spine. Because this muscle group is so close to the spine, one of its jobs is to provide support for it, which is very important during pregnancy. It's common for women to suffer with a bad back whilst pregnant so it's important to carry out this exercise both before and after you give birth. Working it may also help the more superficial abdominal muscles recover sooner.

1. Start on your hands and knees
2. Ensure that your hands are directly under your shoulders and you knees under your hips
3. Your back should be in a flat, neutral position and your head in line with your neck
4. Imagine that you are trying to draw your hip bones together
5. Now draw your navel backwards as if you are trying to make it reach your spine
6. Hold the contraction for as long as possible whilst continuing to breathe normally
7. Relax and repeat up to 10 times

This exercise can be done in any position, seated, lying, standing or kneeling.

ABDOMINAL CURL – 2 SETS OF 15

This exercise works the tummy muscles at the front of your body. However, as discussed earlier, the rectus abdominis muscles experience quite a change during pregnancy. It's important that you start very gradually when exercising this muscle group, and before carrying out the version described below, you should start with small head raises from a lying position before attempting to lift the shoulder blades from the floor. You should also make exercising your pelvic floor a priority over exercising the rectus abdominis. Once you can perform approximately 20 head lifts, you could then progress, but always listen to your body and remember: this muscle group shouldn't be worked until you have had your 'rec check' (see six-week check section).

1. Lie on your back with your legs bent at a 90 degree angle and your feet flat on the floor
2. Place your hands at the sides of your head
3. Curl your head and shoulders, lifting the spine 20 to 30 degrees from the floor
4. Gently lower the head and shoulders back to the starting position in a controlled manner
5. Avoid pulling your head

You can make the exercise easier by placing the arms across the chest, or harder by raising the arms straight up above your head.

FLEXIBILITY

As well as allowing you to move more freely day to day, stretching your muscles can be a very relaxing part of your exercise regimen. Ideally, muscles should only be stretched when they are warm, so do these movements at the end of your workout. Remember, if you are breastfeeding you will still have the hormone relaxin in your system which will make your joints and ligaments more unstable than they used to be, so be careful not to over-do it. Stretches should be held for between 10 to 15 seconds each. If you like attending classes, you should get a nice challenge for your flexibility in classes such as yoga, Pilates and 'stretch and relax'.

Here are the descriptions for some of the main stretches that you can do daily or after carrying out the exercises listed above. However, this is not an exhaustive list and there may be other muscle groups that you would also like to stretch.

HAMSTRING STRETCH (BACK OF YOUR THIGH)

1. Lying on your back, with both legs out straight, raise one leg towards the chest and straighten the knee
2. Hold the back of your thigh
3. Keep your back on the floor
4. Lift the leg towards you to the point where mild tension is felt at the back of the thigh
5. Aim to straighten the knee fully on the stretching leg

QUADRICEPS STRETCH (FRONT OF YOUR THIGH)

1. Lying either on the tummy or on one side, raise one heel towards the buttocks and take hold of the ankle or the foot
2. The bent leg should be in line with the rest of the body
3. Only lift the leg to the point where mild tension is felt on the front of the thigh
4. Tilt the hips slightly forward to increase the stretch

ADDUCTOR STRETCH (INNER THIGH)

1. Sit upright on your sitting bones with either the soles of the feet together or the legs straddled
2. Keep the back straight and the chest lifted
3. Do not allow the body to slump forwards
4. Aim to feel a mild tension on the inside of the thigh

ABDUCTOR STRETCH (OUTSIDE OF THIGH/BUTTOCKS)

1. Lying on your back, place one ankle on the opposite knee
2. Draw the knee into the chest and relax the head and shoulders
3. Feel the stretch on the outside of the hip

This stretch can also be performed in the same way from a seated position.

TRAPEZIUS STRETCH (UPPER BACK)

1. Clasp your hands together in front of you at arm's length
2. Roll the shoulders forwards, separating the shoulder blades
3. Look down between the arms
4. Feel the stretch in the middle of the upper back

PECTORAL STRETCH (CHEST)

1. Place your hands in the small of your back, drawing your elbows together
2. Lift your chest and collar bone without allowing the head to fall backwards
3. Feel the stretch across the front of the body at the chest

Central YMCA Mums' Health Guides

5

LOSING YOUR BABY WEIGHT

If I could complete this book without writing this chapter then I would be happy to do so, but it's the one question on many women's lips after having a baby, so I feel that it's a topic that can't be ignored. Indeed, you may have been fantasising about it whilst you were still pregnant, making plans to get back into your jeans within a couple of months. Perhaps you were the other extreme and thought that you didn't need to worry about weight while you were pregnant and could therefore eat what you wanted, put your feet up and that everything would fall into place after you had your baby. Whatever your position, losing baby weight is something a lot of mums want to achieve, often as quickly as possible.

The simple truth is that during pregnancy, you actually only need to consume approximately 300 additional calories a day from the second trimester. Some women, however, over-eat from the day they find out they are pregnant and consequently gain a large amount of weight, taking them well over the recommended 10 to 13kg weight gain for the full pregnancy.

There is no mystery to this and, put bluntly, if you gain too much weight – or more appropriately, fat – in pregnancy, you will have more to lose afterwards, and at no point in the pregnancy should you be eating for two.

It's important for pregnant women to choose wisely when consuming their additional calories. If you have your extra calories in the form of a chocolate bar, you will not get the same lasting satiety obtained from a more starchy carbohydrate and lean protein snack, such as a jacket potato with tuna. However, when you want chocolate, you want chocolate! It's a cliché but you will do well to accept the fact that it takes nine months to put the weight on, so it will likely take nine months to get it off again. During my pregnancy, I only gained the recommended amount of weight and I thought it would fall off within a week after giving birth. Four months on, I still have 5kg to lose.

If you are breastfeeding your baby, it is recommended that you consume an additional 300 to 500 calories per day. Similarly to pregnancy, choose wisely when it comes to what you eat so that you don't waste your food intake on empty calories. Whilst you are feeding you will inevitably feel very hungry and it's not wise to ignore this by going on a crash diet and worrying about your weight at this time. It can be frustrating as you want to give your baby the best you can, but at the same time, you may feel that want to get your body back after such a long time. If you remember the nine month rule, however, you won't go far wrong. You will also need to ensure you are well hydrated to keep your milk production up, so plenty of water is advisable.

The type of delivery that you had will also have a bearing on how soon you may lose your baby weight. If you had a C-section, you will likely be less mobile than if you had a vaginal delivery, due to the extended recovery period. Therefore, the amount of general daily activity that you carry out will be affected.

Aim to be sensible with your food choices and activity levels and let how you are feeling be a guide. Don't expect to get back to your pre-pregnancy weight for at least nine months and maybe even more if you are breastfeeding for longer as you will continue to need those extra calories. Every woman is different in terms of how quickly she will lose baby weight but you will already have enough on your plate with a new baby, without having the added pressure of changing your body. There will be other times in your life when you can dedicate time to this, but for now, my advice would to just be sensible and kind to yourself.

6

GETTING OUT AND ABOUT

Your first experience of going out after you have had your baby will probably be leaving hospital and, if you are travelling home by car, it may well be one of the most cautious journeys of your life. Most people feel overwhelmed and I remember thinking that the hospital must have made a terrible mistake letting me out to look after this new, tiny, vulnerable creature. Every parent I have spoken to has had a 'What on earth are we supposed to do now?' moment once they have taken their baby home.

I really struggled emotionally in the first few weeks and found that I lost my confidence in doing the most basic things like filling my car up with petrol or doing the weekly shop. I felt too paranoid to go down the fridge and freezer aisles in case my baby froze and would panic if anyone came too close to the pram. After talking to other new mums, I realise that I was in the majority and some people don't leave the house at all for the first few weeks, so it's important that you do what feels manageable for you and try not to compare yourself to others. Small steps are the way forward and I would recommend writing down your daily achievements no matter how simple they seem. My list consisted of things like, 'Went to Tesco and remembered everything that I went for', 'Spoke to two friends on the phone today', and 'I fed and changed the baby by myself'. By looking back on the list I could celebrate what I had achieved instead of feeling down about what I hadn't.

Another recommendation is to mix with other new mums because the chances are they will be experiencing the same feelings you are. By talking and sharing your experiences, you will be assured that you are not going mad and that everything you are feeling is perfectly normal. I realise that some people do not like the idea of mother and baby groups as they feel like they are forcing friendships that wouldn't otherwise exist, but you may be surprised how therapeutic they can be. It doesn't mean you have to be life-long friends who spend all their spare time together, but you can be part of a support network for each other at this time in your life. I have always been a very social person and I love being around people so I knew that going to this kind of group would be inevitable for me. It was a little bit like starting a new job where there are some people that you instantly click with and others that you don't. Surround yourself with the people who support you and who you can support in return, rather than those who make you feel like a failure.

I have already mentioned the benefits of fresh air for both you and your baby, and getting out with the pushchair is a great place to start to exercise the body and the mind. Of course, there may be some barriers to this. It may be that where you live means you need to drive somewhere to get to a walking path. The weather may also be a factor, and you will need sun or rain protection for the pram. And maybe you have other children, so perhaps it's not that easy to take them with you on your walk. The type of delivery you had may also affect your activity levels; long walks shouldn't take place in the first six weeks after a C-section. There will always be barriers, but if getting out and about is important to you, there is usually a way around them that will work.

7

FRIENDS AND FAMILY

Your friends and family will no doubt be eager to meet your new arrival and managing visitors can be quite a challenge when you are tired, hormonal and in pain. However, do not underestimate how much support your friends and family can give you in the early days and beyond.

I am not lucky enough to have family on my doorstep but this doesn't stop my husband's family from frequently visiting and helping me out. In the first few weeks, they would encourage me to go to bed when they arrived so that I could try to catch up on some lost sleep and I strongly believe that this is what kept me going.

Any new mother has to accept that a long block of unbroken sleep is out of the question in the early days, but if you have some help, the odd hour of sleep here and there can certainly keep you sane. It's such a cliché but 'sleep whilst the baby sleeps' is the best advice I can give. I read this in many books before I gave birth and didn't pay much attention to it, but it really is true that the housework and any other jobs can wait. Allow yourself to rest as much as you can without feeling guilty. I got to a stage where I would look forward to people coming over; not to see them, but because I knew I could pop upstairs for a nap whilst they cooed over my baby.

So let us assume you are ready to exercise and need to enlist the help of friends and family whilst you do so. It depends on an individual's opinion of exercise as to whether or not you feel comfortable asking them for help. If your friend doesn't see exercise as a priority in life, asking her to babysit whilst you pop to the gym may be inappropriate, but for the people who know and understand your need to train, it's a perfectly reasonable request. Most people would see it as acceptable to look after your baby whilst you went down the pub for dinner and drinks, so why not whilst you have a workout?

Decide how your support network can help you out. Do you want your friend/family member to look after your baby whilst you exercise? Or maybe you would like them to accompany you on a long walk whilst you run backwards and forwards to lampposts, leaving them in charge of the pram. Perhaps you can set up an arrangement with other mums who are also keen exercisers taking it in turns to workout whilst looking after each other's babies. If you are anything like me, you will feel guilty about doing anything for yourself that doesn't directly benefit your baby, but it's important to remember that if exercising/shopping/meditating or whatever else makes *you* happy, then it will most definitely have a positive effect on your ability to care for your baby. Try to remember that you and your baby are your own people and having time out from each other will benefit you both in the long run.

8

SIGN POSTING

My personal experience of the NHS was a truly fantastic one. My antenatal care was very thorough and the midwives I saw were friendly and approachable. My labour didn't go according to plan as there was meconium in my waters which meant that I had to be continuously monitored, put on a drip and couldn't have the water birth that I wanted, but the midwives in the delivery ward were direct, encouraging and supportive. Before leaving hospital, I was given clear information about what to do in the event of postnatal issues and the home visits in the early days were so helpful. Even now, four months on, the health visitors in my area make it very easy for me to call them if I have any questions or concerns about my baby or myself.

I realise that not everyone's experience will be such a positive one, but be assured that the midwives and health visitors in your area are there to help you. I am still amazed that health visitors can be your point of contact until your child is five years old. You will find that there are plenty of drop-in clinics where you can get your baby weighed and ask for advice. Your health visitor will also be able to inform you of local baby massage and baby yoga courses that you can enrol on, both of which are a fantastic way of bonding with your baby. These courses are also a great opportunity to meet new mums and share your experiences.

The NCT is a great support network too. If you didn't sign up for this whilst you were pregnant, you can do so as a new mum. There are lots of events such as nearly new sales, breastfeeding workshops and coffee mornings that you can attend.

More information can be found on their website, www.nct.org.uk.

I am also grateful to the Royal College of Midwives for its support in the compilation of this book. You can find out more about the incredible work of the RCM and the thousands of inspirational midwives across the UK, whose role is so vital at such a life-changing time for millions of us, at www.rcm.org.uk

You may also be interested to know that there is a free YMCA Mums' Health magazine available for tablets, smartphones and online – it even includes a few videos in which I demonstrate some of the exercises we've discussed here. You can find the magazine in the iTunes store or here:

http://www.pocketmags.com/viewmagazine.aspx?titleid=1270&title=YMCA+Mums'+Health

And lastly, if any of you are interested in finding out more about becoming a personal trainer yourself, then please visit the YMCAfit website – www.ymcafit.org.uk – where you'll find all the information you'll need on how to launch your own career in the fitness industry.

9

GOOD LUCK

I have very much enjoyed writing this book and sharing my own experiences with you, and I hope that in some way it has been of interest and use to you, which was my ultimate goal for it.

There's no doubt that this is the most incredible, life-changing and inspirational time in your life, as well as being the most challenging, tiring and selfless. However, being a mum gets easier with time – or so other mums keep telling me – and I guess this must come down to being increasingly confident in your own mothering abilities as time goes on, and to becoming increasingly in tune with your little one's needs and moods.

Advice at this time is also in ample supply from friends and family, some of it not always of use or relevance. However, if you were to ask me the best advice I could give, it would be to ensure that this is a healthy and happy time; I would pass on the same advice that I was given: trust your instincts and just keep putting one foot in front of the other.

I really believe that, as women, we develop a seventh sense once our babies are born and I feel that it's so important to trust yourself.

Thanks for taking the time to read this book. I wish you years of happiness with your new baby.

See you soon,

Debs

Central YMCA Mums' Health Guides

Discover more books and ebooks of interest to you and find out about the range of work we do at the forefront of health, fitness and wellbeing.

www.ymcaed.org.uk